Colours

Written and illustrated by Satoshi Kitamura

◐ Collins

I went to the art show and I looked at
the paintings.
There were lots of colours in the paintings
and I began to imagine ...

... what if the world was all yellow?
There are lots of different yellows ...

... or what if everything was red?
There are lots of different reds ...

... or what if everything was blue?
Can you imagine a world where
everything is blue?

Then I had an idea.

The world isn't just red or yellow or blue.
It's a mixture of all these colours and
I wanted to try them out.

I went home and I did my own paintings.
Why don't you play with colours, too?
Try out just one, and then add lots more.

A story map

✾ Ideas for guided reading ✾

Learning objectives: Read high frequency words; apply phonic knowledge and skills as the prime approach to reading; identify the main events (beginnings and endings) in stories; use syntax and context when reading for meaning; take turns to speak, listen to others' suggestions and talk about what they are going to do

Curriculum links: Art and Design: Self-portrait; Science: How we see things

High frequency words: and, are, at, can, could, did, had, if, it, just, like, look, more, of, one, or, out, see, the, them, there, to, too, went, were, what, with, would, you

Interest words: colours, art gallery, paintings, imagine, world, different, yellow, red, blue, mixture, green, orange, purple, brow, experiment

Resources: paint, brushes and paper

Word count: 18

Getting started

- Ask the children to name their favourite colour. Ask why they like it. Create a list of all the colours that the children know. Use items in the room to help prompt them. (Note that some children may struggle to see colour.)

- Look at the front cover and read the word *colours* together. What colours can the children see? Read the author's name. Practise blending phonemes to say his name.

- Ask the children to look carefully at the rainbow. What do they know about rainbows? List the colours in the rainbow.

Reading and responding

- Look at p1 together. Discuss where the child is going and what they may see in the art gallery.

- Read pp2–3 together. Model using phonic strategies to decode the word *paintings.*

- Re-read pp2–3 together fluently. Ask them what the child may imagine based on the pictures in the gallery. Encourage them to look closely for detail.

- Read and look at pp4–5 together. What creatures can the children see and where is this picture set? Encourage group discussion.